SOS
NONFICTION COMPANION
TO
Gary Paulsen's
Hatchet

Lisa Kurkov

Rourke
Educational Media

BEFORE, DURING, AND AFTER READING ACTIVITIES

Before Reading: Building Background Knowledge and Academic Vocabulary

Before Reading strategies activate prior knowledge and set a purpose for reading. Before reading a book, it is important to tap into what your child or students already know about the topic. This will help them develop their vocabulary and increase their reading comprehension.

Questions and activities to build background knowledge:
1. Look at the cover of the book. What will this book be about?
2. What do you already know about the topic?
3. Let's study the Table of Contents. What will you learn about in the book's chapters?
4. What would you like to learn about this topic? Do you think you might learn about it from this book? Why or why not?

Building Academic Vocabulary
Building academic vocabulary is critical to understanding subject content.
Assist your child or students to gain meaning of the following vocabulary words.

Content Area Vocabulary
Read the list. What do these words mean?

- aggregate
- boreal
- bush plane
- embedded
- glacier
- Fujita scale
- interdependent
- lean-to
- refraction
- tinder
- waterspouts
- wigwams

During Reading: Writing Component

During Reading strategies help to make connections, monitor understanding, generate questions, and stay focused.
1. While reading, write in your reading journal any questions you have or anything you do not understand.
2. After completing each chapter, write a summary of the chapter in your reading journal.
3. While reading, make connections with the text and write them in your reading journal.
   a) Text to Self – What does this remind me of in my life? What were my feelings when I read this?
   b) Text to Text – What does this remind me of in another book I've read? How is this different from other books I've read?
   c) Text to World – What does this remind me of in the real world? Have I heard about this before? (news, current events, school, etc.)

After Reading: Comprehension and Extension Activity

After Reading strategies provide an opportunity to summarize, question, reflect, discuss, and respond to the text. After reading the book, work on the following questions with your child or students to check their level of reading comprehension and content mastery.
1. What are some survival techniques in the book? (Summarize)
2. Which parts of this book would have been helpful to Brian? (Infer)
3. Have you ever picked berries? What berries do you know that are safe to eat? (Asking Questions)
4. How would you have felt if you were Brian? (Text-to-Self Connection)

Extension Activity
Pick a chapter of the book. With a partner, make a list of things you want to learn more about. Where would you find more information?

TABLE OF CONTENTS

ABOUT *Hatchet* and **Gary Paulsen**

Gary Paulsen is a busy and productive writer. He has written more than 200 books for young people and adults! Three of his novels have received the prestigious Newbery Honor Award. The wilderness is often the setting for Paulsen's novels because it is one of the places where he feels most at home.

In *Hatchet*, Paulsen tells the story of Brian Robeson, a 13-year-old boy flying to visit his dad in Canada. Brian's plane crashes. He spends the next 54 days alone in the Canadian wilderness. Brian battles animals, hunger, and the weather as he figures out what he needs to do to survive.

Author Gary Paulsen

Paulsen, who grew up mostly in northern Minnesota, had a difficult childhood. He ran away as a boy and spent time working on farms, trapping animals, fishing, and living in the woods. He says that he probably slept outdoors more than indoors as a child. Although Paulsen's early life wasn't easy, many of his experiences became subjects for future books.

Just about everything that Brian experiences, Paulsen has too. He survived two forced **bush plane** landings and was even attacked by a moose! *Hatchet*, one of Paulsen's most successful books, took him only four months to write. He claims that all the research was already done—he had lived most of it.

Keep Reading!

If you enjoyed Hatchet, *there are four more books in the Brian series. In the second book,* Brian's Winter, *Paulsen imagines what might have happened if Brian had not been rescued and had to spend the winter in the wilderness. Paulsen hadn't planned on writing a sequel, but he received so many letters from his fans that he eventually wrote an entire series!*

THE CANADIAN NORTH WOODS

From the Novel

Brian is on his way to visit his dad in Canada, but the plane strays off course when the pilot has a heart attack. Brian continues trying to fly the plane for some time, so it is probably several hundred miles off course by the time it crashes.

BOREAL ZONE

ARCTIC
OCEAN

Greenland

Alaska

Yukon

Nunavut

Northwest Territories

British
Columbia

Saskatchewan

HUDSON
BAY

PACIFIC
OCEAN

Alberta

Manitoba

Quebec

Ontario

ATLANTIC
OCEAN

UNITED STATES

The reader doesn't know exactly where Brian's plane crashes, but it somewhere in Canada's North Woods. The Great North Woods is part of an enormous **boreal** zone that stretches around much of the world. This zone occupies more than half of Canada's land area, and the rest extends into the northern United States, Russia, Finland, Denmark, Norway, and Sweden.

In Canada, the North Woods is marked by long, cold, dry winters and short, moist summers. Most of the trees are coniferous, which means they produce cones (like pine trees). There are so many trees in the boreal forest that when they are at their peak in the spring and summer, carbon dioxide levels fall and oxygen levels rise worldwide. This area of Canada is also home to an astounding number of lakes— approximately 1.5 million!

Disturbance in the Woods

It might seem like forest fires, diseases, and insect infestations are dangerous to the health of a forest, but that's not always the case. These disturbances are actually part of the life cycle of boreal forests. For example, fires get rid of dead and dying trees and release nutrients. They thin a forest and let more sunlight in, allowing new growth to take place.

SMALL PLANE BASICS

From the Novel

Brian finds himself flying in a bush plane to visit his father in Canada. It is Brian's first time flying, and he rides in the copilot's seat, impressed by all the dials and switches. The pilot lets him take control for a bit—a stroke of luck for Brian, who must fly the plane after the pilot dies.

BUSH PLANE

Wing

Cockpit

Propeller

Engine

Tail

Rudder

Flap

Elevator

Wing Strut

Fuselage

Pontoon

Landing Gear

A bush plane is a small plane built for flying through and landing in rugged, remote areas. Bush planes often come with equipment like skis or floats that make it possible to land on water, ice, or snow. Typical bush planes have high wings that allow the pilot to land in areas with dense vegetation.

Lucky Landing

Both bush plane forced landings that Paulsen survived took place in Alaska. In the first, the plane's engine suddenly died. Paulsen had no cold-weather clothing or survival gear with him. Luckily, the skilled pilot was able to land the plane on a frozen river using the plane's skis.

Bush planes can land and take off in places where there is no airport—or an airstrip. Bush flying began in the Canadian north. It was a way to transport food, medicine, and building materials to locations that couldn't be reached by roads.

Today's GPS systems make bush flying safer than it once was. In the past, a mistake could easily cost a pilot (and crew) their lives. Bush pilots still need to be skilled in tricky maneuvering and flying at a low speed, which is necessary for takeoffs and landings.

SHELTER

When Brian contemplates building a shelter, his first thought is a **lean-to**. However, he soon finds an area under a ridge that appears to have been scooped out by a **glacier**. He weaves a wall made of sticks and branches to cover most of the opening.

Building or finding shelter is key to survival in the wilderness. Choosing a location is an important decision. Shelters near the water are cooler in warm weather, but they can flood during storms if they are too close.

It's also smart to choose a spot near the available building supplies—otherwise, it takes too much valuable energy to move the materials.

A shelter should be just big enough to lie down inside. It's more work to build a larger shelter, and if the weather is cold, it is easier to conserve body heat in a small space.

Depending on where a person is stranded, there are different options for which shelter is best. Brian's shelter is good for his location. If he were stranded deeper in the forest, he might have made a trench shelter by digging a pit in the ground and using sticks and branches for a roof. If it were to get colder, Brian might have used pine needles and leaves to insulate the floor of his shelter.

Shelter Types

Before Europeans came to North America, indigenous peoples had many different kinds of building traditions. Individual cultures made different styles of homes, and the region's climate played a large role. The Algonquin peoples traveled through much of the eastern boreal forest—where Brian is likely stranded. They preferred conical **wigwams** *that were easy to take down and put back up.*

FORAGING

The first time Brian manages to sate his hunger is when he finds and forages for "gut cherries," as he calls them. He notices a flock of birds and follows them. When he sees them eating berries, he begins shoving them in his mouth as fast as he can.

Foraging for food is tricky, since unfamiliar plants may be poisonous. A small mistake can cause anything from a stomachache and vomiting like Brian experiences, to death. Pine trees are a great source of food. Pine nuts contained in the pinecone are tasty and nutritious. The needles can be used to make tea, and even the inner bark is edible. Unfortunately, they can be easy to confuse with yews, firs, cedars, and cypresses.

A Buggy Snack

The mere thought may make you feel ill, but insects are often edible, available, and nutritious! It's best to cook insects before eating them because they may carry parasites that can make you sick. Ants, grasshoppers, crickets, and even maggots can make a crunchy, tasty snack!

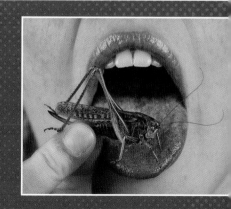

As Brian found out, wild berries are plentiful during the warm months. Blackberries, raspberries, and thimbleberries (similar to raspberries but tarter) are **aggregate** berries and good choices for foragers. A good rule of thumb is to avoid any berry that is found alone on a plant.

Dandelions and cattails are two edible plants that are easy to recognize. Young dandelion leaves taste similar to spinach and are packed with vitamins. Cattails, which you might spot along the edges of a lake or pond, are best in early spring. A forager can eat young stems boiled or raw, and the flower heads are also edible, though not once they are brown and fuzzy.

Plants to Avoid

- *Plants that look like peas or beans*
- *Mushrooms, which are difficult to identify and can be deadly*
- *Plants that have flower clusters shaped like umbrellas*
- *Plants that have sap that changes color when the plant is cut open*
- *Plants with roots that look like garlic, onions, or carrots*

HOW TO START A FIRE

From the Novel

Brian knows that fire is necessary for his survival. He discovers how to start it when he throws his hatchet at the porcupine. He misses the animal, and the hatchet hits a dark, hard stone **embedded** in the cave wall, creating sparks. It's still a while before Brian figures out how to go from sparks to fire, but his persistence pays off.

The necessary elements to build a fire are sparks, **tinder**, fuel, and oxygen. Magnifying glasses, including the lenses in eyeglasses, can focus sunlight and create fire. Using flint and steel, like Brian does, is one of the most reliable methods of making sparks.

Dry grass or leaves will work as tinder. So will paper, lint, rags, or dry bark. The tinder needs to be light and dry to catch easily. It gives the larger pieces of wood a chance to light. Tinder should be at the bottom of a pyramid shape, with larger pieces of wood tented around it. Because a fire needs oxygen to burn, don't pack materials too tightly together.

Once you have a spark, work quickly to use it. Shield it from the wind, and blow gently to encourage it to light the tinder. Do your best not to let your precious fire go out. Remember how much work it was to create!

ANIMALS OF THE
NORTH WOODS

Animals play a major role in Brian's wilderness experience. Some, like bears, wolves, and moose, are a danger to his life, while others, like the skunk, pose a different threat. If an animal is a potential source of food, Brian immediately thinks of ways to hunt or trap it to feed his growling belly.

Like animals worldwide, the creatures of Canada's boreal forest are highly **interdependent**. The snowshoe hare and beaver are two of the most important of the forest's more than 85 mammal species. The hare is a source of food for many predators. The beaver creates dams that flood parts of the woods, forming ponds that serve as a habitat for fish and amphibians, as well as a water source for land animals.

Birds are plentiful in the North Woods. About 3 million birds breed there each year, and approximately 300 million travel through the area during their migration. The ruffed grouses that Brian nicknames "foolbirds" are common year-round, as they don't migrate. Part of their Latin name, Bonasa, means "good when roasted," so Brian isn't the only person to find these plump, chicken-like birds to be tasty!

Put It on Ice

In the boreal forest, most reptiles and amphibians hibernate, as they do in other places where the winters are frigid. Some species of frogs handle the cold a little differently. Instead of hibernating underground, where the temperature stays above freezing, they just burrow into leaf litter. Special chemicals in their bodies keep them from freezing completely, but up to 40 percent of their bodies' liquid can turn to ice!

FISHING

One day, Brian sees a kingfisher dive into the water and emerge with a small fish. Brian is inspired to try his hand at fishing, too, and he's amazed at how many fish he sees. As he soon finds out, catching those fish is another story altogether.

Brian's inability to catch fish in the beginning is because he forgets about refraction. **Refraction** refers to light changing direction. When light travels from air into water, it slows down, which causes what you see to shift or bend. Brian aims where he thinks he sees fish. But because of refraction, his aim is not accurate. Only when he figures this out does he begin to catch his dinner!

refraction

One good thing about fish is that they are all edible. Some will
taste better than others, but any kind of fish can make a meal.
There are about 130 species of fish in Canada's boreal forest. They
tend to be hardy types of fish, such as minnows, walleye, lake trout,
yellow perch, and northern pike, because they need to survive long,
harsh winters.

Plastic Bottle Fish Trap

To make a fish trap from a plastic bottle, cut two inches off the top. Place pebbles in the bottle to weigh it down. Turn the cut-off piece upside down and push it into the opening of the bottle. Place the trap in shallow water. Minnows will swim in but won't be able to swim out. They are useful as bait for larger fish.

TORNADO!

From the Novel

The low roar of the tornado alerts
Brian to what is happening. He has
no time to prepare—he can only react. The tornado tosses
Brian around, slamming him into the walls of his shelter. It
takes most of his meager possessions, but also makes the
plane visible in the water, which ultimately leads to
Brian's rescue.

A tornado is a rotating column of air that stretches from the sky to the ground. It may touch the ground only for a moment, or it may travel for miles, causing great destruction. The strength of a tornado can vary greatly. Scientists measure tornadoes using the **Fujita scale**, or F-scale. They rate tornadoes from F0 to F5, which is the strongest type.

Waterspout

*There are two types of **waterspouts**—fair weather waterspouts and tornadic waterspouts. Fair weather waterspouts move from the surface of the water upwards, the opposite of tornadic spouts. Tornadic spouts form under the same conditions that land tornadoes do. They look like a whirling funnel column over a body of water and rarely move inland.*

WILDERNESS RESCUE

From the Novel

When Brian wakes up after his crash landing, he's convinced that he will be found very soon. Maybe by the end of the day, or three days later at the most. Brian is eventually rescued after 54 days by a pilot who purchases furs from the Cree trapping camps.

Search and rescue (SAR) teams use many techniques to find and save people in danger. They are responsible for responding to natural and human-made disasters, as well as downed planes and sinking boats. In missing persons cases, the first priority is establishing a search area. This can be where someone was last seen, or in the case of a downed plane, the route it was supposed to take.

Because Brian's plane drifted so far off course, the SAR teams looking for him were in the wrong spot.

The pilot who finds Brian is able to do so because he picks up an emergency signal. Emergency locator transmitters are airplane staples. They send distress signals over a specific frequency. Paulsen does not give a year for when *Hatchet* takes place, but he wrote it in the 80s. During that time, transmitters on planes operated at lower frequencies that were only detectable by ground support and aircraft flying directly overhead.

Brian's transmitter was also a manual one. Many modern devices now activate on impact or by a remote switch in the cockpit. If Brian were lost today, he would likely be found much faster with the technological advances in place!

MIC

LOUDSPEAKER

EMERGENCY LOCATOR TRANSMITTER
PERSONAL LOCATOR BEACON:
WARNING! FOR EMERGENCY USE ONLY

121.5 / 243 / 406 MHz
WITH SPEECH, ON UHF & VHF

CLASS 2 (-20°C to +55°C
JTSO-2C91a & JTSO-2C126
TSO-C91a & TSO-C126

OPERATING INSTRUCTIONS
ROTATE ANTENNA 150° AND EXTEND

PULL LANYARD / SLIDE SWITCH
DOWN TO ACTIVATE BEACON

SLIDE SWITCH UPWARDS TO
ACTIVATE BUILT IN TEST (BIT)
UNTIL S....G IS SHOWN

BUILT IN TEST (B.I.T) STATUS

CONT ON:	PLB OPERATIONAL
FAST FLASH:	BATTERY FAILURE
SLOW FLASH	
FLASH WITH	INTERNAL FAULT
PAUSE	

Emergency locator transmitters aren't the only way of calling for help! Flashlights and bonfires can both be used for signaling. Brian attempts this early in the story. Boats, planes, or even other people on the ground can see the signal and investigate. Large ground signals, such as SOS or HELP, can also be written using branches, snow, or sand for passing aircraft to see. Humans have created and developed many different ways of hailing help and surviving no matter where they are stranded.

Lost and Found

In 2007, a 12-year-old Boy Scout became lost in the North Carolina woods while camping with his troop. The Boy Scout, Michael Auberry, had read Hatchet *a couple of years before, and his father credits the book with helping Michael avoid panicking. The resourceful scout drank river water (hoping he wouldn't get sick) and slept in tree branches. He was found after four days by a rescue dog team.*

DISCUSSION QUESTIONS

1. How does Gary Paulsen's early life influence his writing?

2. Explain how a bush plane differs from a regular plane.

3. Do you like Paulsen's idea of continuing the story in *Brian's Winter* and imagining a different ending? Why or why not?

4. What effect does the boreal forest as a whole have on the world?

5. What role does the beaver play in the boreal forest?

6. Describe several ways you might be able to attract rescuers' attention if you were lost in the wilderness.

7. Imagine what kind of shelter you would have made if you were lost. Do some research on different types of shelters and compare them to Brian's. Would you make something different? Why or why not?

WRITING PROMPTS AND PROJECTS

1. Do some research about eating bugs. What are the benefits for humans and the environment? In what cultures is this already common? How do you feel about it personally?

2. If you packed a survival kit, what would you include in it and why?

3. Describe a natural setting that is familiar to you. It could be your backyard, a park, or a place you've gone hiking. If you were stranded there and could only bring five items with you, what would you bring and why?

4. Make a diorama of Brian's wilderness.

   • Suggested materials: a shoebox or other medium-sized box, paint, construction paper, clay, branches, rocks, moss or dried grass, craft sticks, animal figures (if you have them)

   • Create a scene from the novel. Use as many details as you can from the book to recreate a little part of Brian's world.

GLOSSARY

aggregate (AG-ri-git): clustered together

boreal (BAWR-ee-uhl): relating to or located in the north

bush plane (buhsh pleyn): a type of plane that flies into areas of wild land with heavy vegetation

embedded (im-BED-ed): tightly surrounded or enclosed

Fujita scale (FOO-jee-ta skeyl): a scale used for rating the strengths of tornadoes, based on the amount of damage they cause

glacier (GLEY-sher): a large mass of ice moving very slowly through a valley or down a slope

interdependent (in-ter-di-PEN-duhnt): depending on one another

lean-to (leen-too): a structure with a sloped roof and one side supported by a tree, posts, or other object

refraction (ruh-FRAK-shn): the change in direction of a wave (light, radio, etc.) passing from one medium to another

tinder (TIN-der): dry material that burns easily, like wood or paper; used to start a fire

waterspouts (WAW-ter-spouts): a spinning funnel column above a body of water

wigwams (WIG-wahms): dome-shaped huts or tents made by fastening mats, skins, or bark over a framework of poles

BIBLIOGRAPHY

Bishop, Charles A., Zach Parrot. "Eastern Woodlands Indigenous Peoples in Canada," The Canadian Encyclopedia. December 21, 2017. https://www.thecanadianencyclopedia.ca/en/article/aboriginal-people-eastern-woodlands. (accessed June 22, 2020).

British Columbia Adventure Network. http://www.bcadventure.com/adventure/wilderness/survival/basic.htm. (accessed June 3, 2020).

Canadian Wildlife Federation. https://www.hww.ca/en/wild-spaces/boreal-forest.html. (accessed June 5, 2020).

David Suzuki Foundation. https://davidsuzuki.org/project/boreal-forest/. (accessed June 9, 2020).

Gadacz, René R, Michelle Filice. "Wigwam," The Canadian Encyclopedia. May 19, 2020. https://bit.ly/31NCIZD. (accessed June 20, 2020).

Long, Denise. *Survivor Kid: A Practical Guide to Wilderness Survival*. Chicago: Chicago Review Press Inc., 2011.

Paulsen, Gary. *Guts: The True Stories Behind Hatchet and the Brian Books*. New York: Laurel-Leaf Books, 2001. ——— *Hatchet*. New York: Simon & Schuster Books for Young Readers, 1987.

Pitts, Jonathan. "Novel Might Have Helped Save Missing Scout's Life," The Baltimore Sun, March 21, 2007. https://www.baltimoresun.com/news/bs-xpm-2007- 03-21-0703210263-story.html. (accessed June 6, 2020).

INDEX TERMS

ABOUT THE AUTHOR

Lisa Kurkov lives in Charlotte, North Carolina, where she and her husband homeschool their two children. When her head isn't buried in a book, Lisa enjoys baking, crafting, photography, birding, and adventuring with her family.

www.rourkeeducationalmedia.com

PHOTO CREDITS: page 1: roundex/Shutterstock.com; page 2: nopow/Getty Images; page 4: petrmalinak/Shutterstock.com; page 6: Brian Baer/ZUMAPRESS/Newscom; page 6: Lemon_tm/Getty Images; page 6: ehrlif/Getty Images; page 7: den-belitsky/Getty Images; page 8: Gregory_DUBUS/Getty Images; page 8: Mehmet Hilmi Barcin/Getty Images; page 8: imageBROKER/Gerhard Zwerger-Schoner/Newscom; page 9: forest_strider/Getty Images; page 10: Pgiam/Getty Images; page 11: Byronsdad/Getty Images; page 12: Gregory_DUBUS/Getty Images; page 12: NNehring/Getty Images; page 13: PressedDesigns/Getty Images; page 13: a_Taiga/Getty Images; page 14: Josh Anon/Shutterstock.com; page 15: Ballun/Getty Images; page 15: BardoczPeter/Getty Images; page 16: PhoThoughts/Getty Images; page 16: kmatija/Getty Images; page 17: marcduf/Getty Images; page 18: Ysbrand Cosijn/Shutterstock.com; page 19: Steve_Bramall/Getty Images; page 20: RLSPHOTO/Getty Images; page 20: AVTG/Getty Images; page 21: RedHelga/Getty Images; page 21: Anest/Getty Images; page 21: chengyuzheng/Getty Images; page 21: MauMyHaT/Getty Images; page 22: Avalon_Studio/Getty Images; page 22: wingmar/Getty Images; page 23: Usercce650b4_975/Getty Images; page 23: Tolga TEZCAN/Getty Images; page 24: Lebazele/Getty Images; page 24: Pavel L Photo and Video/Shutterstock.com; page 24: Igor Meynson/Getty Images; page 25: mrgao/Getty Images; page 25: vitrolphoto/Shutterstock.com; page 26: Alikaj2582/Getty Images; page 27: BrilliantEye/Getty Images; page 28: rpbirdman/Getty Images; page 29: stanley45/Getty Images; page 30: Tom Reichner/Shutterstock.com; page 31: jdwfoto/Getty Images/Getty Images; page 31: Donyanedomam/Getty Images; page 32: Tong_stocker/Shutterstock.com; page 32: BrendanHunter/Getty Images; page 33: combomambo/Getty Images; page 34: abadonian/Getty Images; page 35: stammphoto/Getty Images; page 36: Perszing1982/Getty Images; page 36: nickalbi/Getty Images; page 37: Minerva Studio/Shutterstock.com; page 37: ergregory/Getty Images; page 38: Chalabala/Getty Images; page 39: leezsnow/Getty Images; page 40: depaz/Shutterstock.com; page 41: depaz/Shutterstock.com; page 42: photopixel/Shutterstock.com; page 42: Chainarong Prasertthai/Getty Images; page 43: hxdbzxy/Shutterstock.com; page 43: scaliger/Getty Images; page 44: Marcelo Silva/Getty Images; cover: MaximFesenko/Getty Images; cover: fergregory/Getty Images; cover: Tolga TEZCAN/Getty Images; cover: Julia_Sudnitskaya/Getty Images; cover: photo5963/Getty Images; cover: petrmalinak/Shutterstock.com; cover: photopixel/Shutterstock.com; cover: DavidTB/Shutterstock.com; page n/a: enjoynz/Getty Images; page n/a: -slav-/Getty Images

Library of Congress PCN Data

Nonfiction Companion to Gary Paulsen's Hatchet / Lisa Kurkov
(Nonfiction Companions)
ISBN 978-1-73164-342-1 (hard cover)
ISBN 978-1-73164-306-3 (soft cover)
ISBN 978-1-73164-374-2 (e-Book)
ISBN 978-1-73164-406-0 (e-Pub)
Library of Congress Control Number: 2020945082

Rourke Educational Media
Printed in the United States of America
01-3502011937

Edited by: Madison Capitano
Cover and interior design by: Joshua Janes